# Foreign Exchange Trading for Absolute Beginners

Getting Started In FX Trading – A Beginners Guide

# Contents

## Disclaimer of Warranty / Limits of Liability

# Chapter 1 – The Foreign Exchange Trading for Absolute Beginners

What exactly is FOREX trading? Put simply, FOREX trading is the buying and selling of international currencies. Traditionally, participation in the FOREX market was confined to major banking and trading institutions. But in recent years, technological developments have opened up this once exclusive arena to smaller companies and even individuals by allowing them to trade currencies online.

The world's currency rates are not fixed. They follow a floating exchange rate and are always traded in pairs— Eur Dollar, Dollar/Yen, etc. Most international transactions are exchanges of the world's major currencies.

**FOREIGN EXCHANGE CONCEPT & INVESTMENT TOOLS**

1. SPOT FOREX TRADING – Spot trading is one of the most common types of forex trading. A spot transaction is a two-day delivery transaction as opposed to futures contracts which are usually three months. The Spot trade represent a direct exchange between two currencies, has a short time frame, involves cash rather than a contract and interest is not included in the agreed upon transaction.

2. FORWARD FOREX TRADING – Once way to deal with the foreign exchange risk is to engage in a forward transaction. Money does not actually change hands in this type of transactions, until some agreed upon future date. The buyer and seller agree on an exchange rate for any date in the future and the transaction occurs on that date. The duration of the trade could be one day, a few days, months or years.

3. SWAP FOREX TRADING – The most common type of forward contracts is the FX swaps. In a swap, two parties exchange currencies for a certain length of time and agree to reverse the transaction at an agreed upon future date. The swap transactions are not standardized contracts and are not traded through an exchange.

4. FUTURES FOREX TRADING – these are standardized forward contracts an unlike swap trades and usually traded on an exchange. The average contract length is roughly three months and usually the contracts are inclusive of any interest amounts. Currency futures contracts are contracts specifying a

standard volume of a specific currency to be exchanged on a specific belittlement date.

5. OPTION FOREX TRADING – A FX option is a derivative where the owner has the right but not the obligation to exchange money denominated in one currency into another currency at a pre-agreed exchange rate on a specified date.

When it comes to Forex trading, there are a number of major currency pairs.: Euro v. US dollar, US dollar v. Japanese yen, British pound v. US dollar, and US dollar v. Swiss franc. These currency pairs are considered major in comparison to the other currency pairs because of their trading volume.

In the FOREX market, these relationships are shortened: EUR/USD, USD/JPY, GBP/USD, and USD/CHF. They may also be listed as follows (without the slash): EURUSD, USDJPY, GBPUSD, and USDCHF

Below is a chart of 4 currency pairs clearly illustrating their relationship to each other.

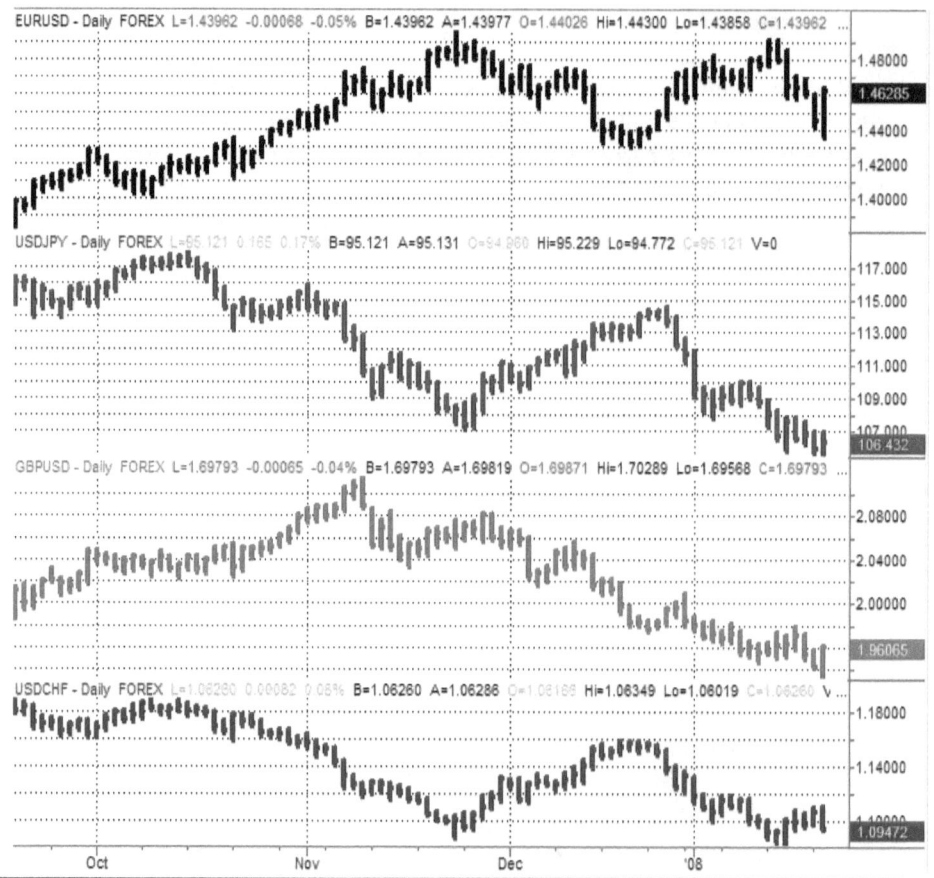

**Figure 1.0 Major Currency Pairs – Daily Data**

It is also important to remember that there are no dividends paid on currencies. If you are a trader in the FOREX market, you look to see whether one currency's value will appreciate against another currency. When this is the case, you exchange the latter for the first. Ideally, you will be able to exchange the first currency for the other at a later time and collect a profit from the trade.

FOREX transactions are typically conducted by professionals at major banks and brokerage firms. FOREX trading has long been an important feature of the international market. At all hours of the day, currencies are being traded by brokers around the world. In fact, the FOREX market operates virtually twenty four hours a day and five days a week with traders at international banking institutions working a number of separate shifts.

The FOREX market is different from the normal stock market in the fact that price shifts are much smoother and do not result in significant gaps. Each day the FOREX market turns over trillions of dollars, allowing traders to enter and exit certain position very easily. As you can see, the FOREX market is a dynamic and continuous system that basically never sleeps.

Also known as the foreign exchange market, or FX, it is the oldest and most expansive financial market in the world. In comparison, the currency futures market is a mere one percent the size of the FOREX market. Currency futures are an exchange-traded futures contract that specify the price in one currency at which another currency can be bought or sold at a future date. Currency futures can be used to hedge other trades or currency risks, or to speculate on price movements in currencies. But we will not delve much into currency future in this basic guide.

Trades are brokered between major banking groups and circulate around the globe, from America to Australia, to Asia, to Europe, and back to the U.S. For a long time, financial prerequisites and hefty minimum transaction amounts put the FOREX market out of reach of small traders. Consequently, at one time major banks and financial institutions were the only parties that could benefit from participation in the FOREX market's fluidness and strong exchange rates.

Today is a different story. FOREX market dealers can divide large units within the market, allowing smaller corporations and even individuals the ability to trade these smaller units. Even though it is the oldest financial market in the world, the FOREX market has evolved a great deal in a short amount of time. High-speed internet connections and sophisticated online Forex trading platforms has definitely made it easier for individual traders to get involved in Forex trading and possibly be very successful at it. This basic guide is your first step towards a successful future in trading in the extremely lucrative FOREX market.

### Reasons To Trade In The FOREX Market

If you asked Forex traders the number one reason, they traded Forex most of them would say, **"profit potential"**

**Figure 1.1 Daily GBPUSD Data**

The chart above shows the daily GBPUSD (British Pound/US Dollar) currency pair. This chart shows the "**BUY**" entry where the blue arrow is (the bottom left of the chart). This represents where a particular Forex trading system went long (bought).

The profit so far in this trade is approximately $24,000 per Forex contract. This is from just one simple trade in the Forex market! So, as you can see the profit potential is there and opportunities such as these exist in all Forex currency pairs.

There is a unique and potentially very profitable opportunity offered through cash/spot FOREX markets regardless of the condition of the market.

**The advantages of FOREX trading are:**

**Around the clock market:** A trader can trade anytime that they think market conditions are favorable; Forex offers a 24-hour market. This is particularly convenient for those who wish to trade Forex on a part-time basis. You could easily find markets to trade that will not conflict with your work schedule. There is basically no schedule that the Forex market's trading hours can't accommodate.

**Easy in-Easy out:** A trader can enter or exit the market almost totally at will; no other market offers as much liquidity. There are very few execution barriers and no limits are placed on daily trading. The leverage available in Forex is much higher than equity markets: A leverage ratio of up to 400:1 in comparison to 2:1 in the equity markets.

Although the risk of using greater leverage can be higher in FOREX trading, the potential for profit is there as well!

**A low-cost transaction:** Compared to other markets the Forex market has some of the lowest transaction costs available.

**Always An Opportunity To Profit:** FOREX trading actually consists of buying or selling one currency against another, and there is always a profit opportunity for one currency pair or another.

**Global market:** With no organized exchanges like the New York Stock Exchange, trading is facilitated by electronic communication and telephones.

**No market monopoly:** Because of the size of the FOREX market, no single trader or bank can control the market price for any length of time. Because of the ineffectiveness of bank interventions to manipulate prices, they have diminished.

**It is basically unregulated:** There are no specific FOREX regulations for daily operations. Of course, banks are always regulated through banking laws.

**There are many different advantages to trading FOREX instead of futures or stocks, such as:**

**1. Lower Margin** - A FOREX trader can control a large amount of currency with only a small account deposit, just like when futures and stock speculation is done. Futures require a 5% margin and the margin required for FOREX is around 1%. In layman's terms, in FOREX trading, a currency trader can control 5 times as much with his money as in futures trading and 50 times more than stock trading!

There is much profit in trading on margin, but you need to be fully aware of the very high risks too. Be sure you understand the ins and outs of your margin account and that you have read the margin agreement between you and the clearing firm. If you still have things you are not sure about, discuss these issues beforehand with your account representative.

If you allow your account to fall below an amount set in your agreement, you could experience the partial or complete liquidation of your positions. It may be done before you even get a margin call, so be sure you review your margin balance regularly.

Take advantage of stop-loss orders on each open position; this is a must in order to reduce risk and preserve valuable working capital. A stop-loss order is simply an order placed with a broker to buy or sell once the stock reaches a certain price. A stop-loss is intended to limit an investor's loss on a FX position. Stop loss orders are most effective at halting trades when severe markets dips make returns to profitability unlikely. Its is considered one of trickiest concepts in forex trading.

**2. There are No Exchange Fees and NO Commission** - You pay exchange and brokerage fees in the futures market which are standardized futures contracts to buy or sell currency at a set date, time, and contract size. These contracts are traded at one of the numerous futures exchanges around the world. ... This settlement price is then used to determine whether a gain or loss has been incurred in a futures account. But the FOREX trading is commission free with most Forex brokers. You benefit from free access to this worldwide network where buyers and sellers are matched almost instantly. Although the trading is commission free, the spread (difference between the asking price and the bidding price) is larger than futures.

**3. Guaranteed Stops and Limiting Risk** – Unlike the sometimes unlimited risk involved in the futures market, FOREX is said to have guaranteed stops that can be utilized to limit risk. This is a myth. During a time of extreme volatility your stops in the Forex market can be "run" just as in any other market. We personally know of a trader with one of the largest Forex brokerages who had his stops run by over 140 pips per contract! Basically it is the equivalent of not being able to get out of a futures trading position as the price moves against you.

You are able to plan ahead to limit risk to some degree in the FOREX trading market. An example of this would be losses sustained in the futures market due to Mad Cow Disease.

**4. Trade Rollover In FOREX trading**, you need to rollover each trade every two days just to keep your position. In futures, you must plan ahead to rollover when a contract expires.

**5. Open Around the Clock** – In the futures market your trading is limited during the window of time that each market is open. If current events make getting out of a position important, you still must wait until the market reopens. That could be hours, creating financial disaster for you. But the FOREX market is open around the clock, five days a week. It actually follows the sun! From Europe, to the United States, to Asia, Australia, and back again to the States, it allows you to trade at any time you desire.

**6. A Market place of Free Trade On a daily basis**, the foreign exchange is a $1.4 trillion (and growing) dollar market! This is 46 times larger than all the futures markets combined. Governments around the world struggle to control their own currency because of the massive number of people trading FOREX worldwide.

FOREX trading is a tremendous opportunity and an alternative to futures and commodities trading. As is true with all trading, there are certainly risks involved. To reduce your risk, the services of a Broker are important and advised. This comprehensive guide will help you learn what is necessary to achieve success in the FOREX market. Let's get started!

## Chapter 2 – Getting Started In The Exciting World Of Forex Trading

Learning to trade with Forex is not unnecessarily difficult; however, there are definitely a few items you must be aware of and instructions to follow. Before beginning any trading, obviously you need to locate and forge a relationship with a broker to execute the trades. Just as with doctors, lawyers and other professions, there are a multitude of Forex brokers from which you can select.

**To help you choose, here are some factors to consider:**

**Minimal Spreads** - Unlike standard stock trading brokers, Forex brokers do not charge any commissions on the trades. They earn their income from what is called a spread. The spread is simply the difference between the buy and sell price of currency at a particular point in time. As you locate and investigate the brokers, you should inquire as to the spreads they charge. The lower the spread, the less it will cost you to trade in Forex. This is the same rule as with traditional brokers. The higher their commission on the trades, the lower your profit at the conclusion of the buy and sell transaction. It is in your best interest to choose a Forex broker offering a low spread.

**Compliance and Reputation** - Traditional stock trading brokers generally operate through their own brokerage houses. Forex brokers, however, are most often affiliated with a large bank or other financial institution. This is due to the substantial sums of capital required. In addition, you should confirm that the Forex broker you choose is properly licensed and registered. Forex brokers should be registered with the Futures Commission Merchant (FCM). In addition, they are regulated by the Commodity Futures Trading Commission (CFTC).

You can locate and verify the registration as well as other facts and background information at the CFTC website at http://www.cftc.gov .Without a doubt, you want to retain and trade through a broker who is affiliated with a reputable bank or financial institution.

**Available Research Tools and Information** - Like traditional stock and commodity brokers, Forex brokers maintain various types of websites, trading platforms and underlying research and information portals. The sites should provide you with real time information, current charts, technical information and comparison ability and other relevant data.

A good Forex trader will also sustain the ability to trade on different systems. As with any major financial endeavor of this type, ask for free trials so you can evaluate the Forex broker's various trading platforms. Forex brokers should offer a wide array of information, schedules, tools and other support functions and records.

The bottom line is to locate a broker who will provide you with all the tools and services you require to be successful.

**A Variety Of Leverage Options** – To succeed in Forex trading you Leverage the price spreads on your trades. The price differentials are minute down to the small percentages of a penny. You are, however, using more than your actual capital borrowed from the broker to make the trades which is how you Leverage larger amounts for your trades than you actually have in cash. This allows you to earn money on the small price deviations.

As an example, if you are leveraging at a ration of 100 to 1, this means that for every one of your dollars with which you are trading, you are borrowing 100 from the broker. A wide majority of brokers will allow you to leverage up to a 250 to 1 ratio.

You need to be careful, however, because the leverage ratio is directly related to risk. The higher the ratio, the more you are effectively borrowing from the broker. While you can earn more profit from the trades, you can also lose more if the price fluctuation is not in your favor. This risk reward evaluation is based on your own capital amounts and your tolerance level for profits and losses on the trades.

If you are flush with capital, leveraging a higher amount is not as much of a concern. Nevertheless, brokers offer a large number of leveraging ratios and you will certainly find one or more to fit your desires and financial constraints. Even if you have a good amount of capital and can accept a certain amount of risk, you may not want to leverage a high amount if the market becomes volatile such as with exotic currency pairs.

**Types of Accounts** – You will need to open an account with a broker to execute trades. There are a variety of types of accounts which you can maintain. The lowest account is referred to as a mini account. It has a low minimum opening balance requirement of approximately $300.00. A mini account provides you with the highest ratio of leverage since you are using a small amount of capital with which to execute larger sums in your trades.

Aside from the mini account is a standard account. That type of account provides a multitude of various leverage ratios. It has a higher minimum balance to open of approximately $2,000.00.

Finally, another type of account which brokers offer is a premium account. These require substantially higher minimums to open. They also offer you multiple ratios of leverage as well as give you access to additional platforms, tools and services. As you evaluate and pick a broker, find one that has the right mix of accounts, leverage, information and services for your requirements and financial circumstances.

**Stay Away From Disreputable Brokers** - Just like in any profession, there are good and bad representatives. Brokers are no different. Some are reputable and others are the ones you just need to avoid. These are the brokers who do not have your best interest in hand and simply buy prematurely or sell near a preset price point to increase their own profits.

These brokers will pick up a fraction of a penny always against on your trades. None of the brokers you evaluate will ever admit to such trading, but there are methods to determine if you are considering a broker who engages in this practice.

You can speak with other brokers to get their opinion on the one or more that you are considering. You can ask if they are aware of the brokers trading proclivity in terms of the buying and selling near the price points.

There is no organization that tracks this type of activity. You can try to look on the Internet for discussion boards or messages that might disclose certain brokers and their trading activity.

**Margin Calls and Requirements** - Obviously since leveraging is all about borrowing money from the broker you need to understand exactly how much risk your broker is going to allow you to take on trades.

Once you establish that together and discuss it, the broker will know the prices and differentials in the fluctuations within which to trade by buying or selling. This can, however, adversely impact you if the broker has that discretion and trades at losses.

For example, assume you maintain a margin account and your positions dramatically fall before turning around and rising substantially even exceeding the beginning price. Whether or not you have sufficient capital, a broker might have traded out your position during the fall to lessen the broker's risk and potential loss. That trade could have been at or near the bottom of the price fluctuation. That would result in a margin call to you and you could be liable for substantial sums of money even though the price rebounded after the broker liquidated your position.

Opening a Forex account, regardless of the type, is similar to taking out a rotating equity loan or maintaining an equity account. The main thing that separates them from the Forex account is that you are required to execute a margin agreement with relation to your Forex accounts.

The margin agreement acknowledges that you are trading with money borrowed from the broker and that the broker can insert itself into your trades as necessary to lower its risk and protect its interest. It also explains your liability relating to any losses. After you execute the agreement and deposit the initiating capital to the account you opened, you are ready to begin trading.

# Chapter 3 - Overview of Basic FOREX Strategy

Technical analysis and fundamental analysis are considered the two main forms of analysis in both the FOREX market as well the equity markets. However, most FOREX traders opt for using technical analysis.

The following is a quick overview of both types of analysis and how they are used in FOREX trading.

**Fundamental Analysis**

Fundamental analysis is a way of looking at the forex market by analyzing economic, social, and political forces that may affect the supply and demand of an asset. To do this, fundamental traders study macro-economic indicators and data that is published regularly at particular times by governmental agencies and the private sector. Understanding fundamental macro analysis and the key indicators that traders work with including the labor market, economic growth, trade, housing data and retail sales. The idea behind this type of analysis is that if a country's current or future economic outlook is good, their currency should strengthen. Fundamental analysis is about observing the intrinsic value of an investment, its function in forex entails looking at the economic conditions that affect the valuation of a country's currency.

Using fundamental analysis in the FOREX market tends to be somewhat difficult and is generally used to forecast long-terms trends. There are, of course, some traders who conduct their trades on a short-term basis solely on current news releases. There are many fundamental indicators of currency values that are released at various times so we have provided a list of a few for you to be aware of:

- Non-farm Payrolls
- Purchasing Managers Index or PMI
- Consumer Price Index or CPI
- Retail Sales · Durable Goods

Of course, these are not the only fundamental indicators you need to be aware of. There are also several meetings that can provide you with additional information that may affect a market. These meetings usually focus on interest rates, inflation, and other causes of currency value fluctuation. Sometimes a volatile market is caused by something as simple as the wording of issues such as the Federal Reserve chairman's discussion on interest rates.

The most significant meetings you should be aware of are the Federal Open Market Committee and Humphrey Hawkins Hearings. Simply studying the commentary can help FOREX fundamental analysts to better understand long-terms market trends and can also help short-term traders capitalize on the market.

Should you opt for the fundamental strategy, you should keep an economic calendar on hand so you know when these reports are available. Your broker should be able to keep you up-to-date on this information as well.

Above is sum up of the fundamental analysis. For those like to know more, please read on.

Fundamental analysis is a way of looking at the forex market by analyzing economic social and political forces that may affect the supply and demand of an asset now in other words fundamental analysis is a way of analyzing potential moves of a currency through the strength or weakness of that country's economic outlook.

To do this however fundamental traders study macroeconomic indicators data which is published regularly at a particular time by governmental agencies and the private sector now key figures include data releases on the country's labor market economic growth and trade as well as sectoral releases such as housing data or retail sales figures fundamental traders follow these data releases and news announcements religiously this is because in order to piece together the bigger picture of a currency strength they use this in relation to other countries more to the point these events can represent great trading opportunities.

Now after the publication of these indicators, traders will observe the volatility of the markets however the degree of volatility is really determined depending on the importance of the indicator which is why it's important to actually understand which indicators are important and what they actually represent. Naturally data out of the U.S. tends to have the biggest impact on the financial markets simply because the U.S. is as we know the world's biggest economy.

To take a closer look in more detail at the economic data releases that matter most. Interest rate announcements play the most important role in moving the prices of currencies in the forex markets and as institutions that set interest rates central banks are the great movers of markets. The interest rates dictate flows of investment and the supply and demand of a nation's currency which is exactly why when central bank's change interest rates they cause the forex market to experience movement and volatility and in the realm of forex trading accurate speculation of central bank's actions can enhance the traders chances for a successful trade. When central bank's change their interest rates they are also changing the economic environment so a cut or raise in interest rates is always something traders are on the lookout for.

Alongside interest rate changes, any drastic changes in a central bank's monetary policy including a hint or announcement of non-conventional central bank actions like quantitative easing (QE) will likely call some wild swings in the financial markets especially the forex market.

In general a rate rise will usually cause that economy's currency to strengthen on the other hand a rate cut or extreme measures such as asset purchases will cause that economy's currency to usually weaken gross domestic product commonly referred to as GDP is one of the primary indicators to gauge the health of a country's economy and it represents the total market value of all goods and services produced in the country during the year.

If the GDP figure is growing it means that country's economy is doing better and in turn if it is decreasing or slowing it means the country itself is making less money and is becoming less competitive.

Since a GDP figure itself is often considered a lagging indicator most forex traders focus on the two reports that are issued in the months before the final GDP figures that's the advance report and the preliminary report now importantly here significant revisions between these reports can cause some significant volatility.

Inflation is another prime indicator of the economic state of a country's economy now the Consumer Price Index or CPI is probably the most crucial indicator of inflation it represents the changes in the level of retail prices for a basket of typical goods and services now if the prices for the basic consumer basket is increasing that means inflation is also increasing.

Remember inflation is tied directly to the purchasing power of the currency so if the economy develops in normal conditions the increase in inflation can and technically should lead to that country's central bank increasing basic interest rate which in turn leads to an increase in the attractiveness of a currency. However, in a time when many major central banks are embarking on QE to stimulate the economy it is not always strictly the case.

Employment data is also a major indicator as it reflects the overall health of an economy or business cycle. In order to actually understand how an economy is functioning it is important to know how many jobs are being created what percentage of the workforce is actively working and exactly how many people are claiming unemployment benefits. U.S. non-farm payrolls (U.S. NFP) is arguably one of the most important data releases published. In theory a good beat from NFP should strengthen the US dollar unless it is significantly below market view.

Trade balance the producer price index and other indicators such as the purchasing managers index and industrial production are all important data releases that all measure production and demand. If a country's goods are in high demand that same country's currency will also be in high demand.

The key is to find and interpret data points in the report that are relevant to the overall currency trends and apply them when initiating a position. Since the US trade balance is usually closely watched globally, it is therefore used as an example when considering a long-term position forex. Traders should always review the data of the US trade balance report simultaneously when looking at other important data points for example like consumer prices GDP and of course the Federal Reserve rate announcements.

Short term investors will consider the trade balance report as it relates to market sentiment using the report as a reason to either buy or sell a position in the currency. If we take industrial production figures as another example as with most of the other fundamental indicators the markets will actually already have perceived consensus. A consensus number before the release meaning that if the difference is larger or worse than expected the bond markets will react in the short-term.

Central releases such as retail sales and housing data are also important to keep an eye on. Retail sales data is released on a monthly basis and is important to forex traders as it shows the overall strength of consumer spending and the success of retail stores as well as consumer demand sentiment which indicates broad consumer spending patterns and in turn the immediate health or direction of an economy house and age.

On the other hand, it is one of the most important areas that affect the decision to increase maintain or cut interest rates by a central bank for example expectations of an interest rate cut in the UK would require evidence of a slowdown in housing price increases

If you're a trader trading the British Pound you would watch the UK housing data and retail sales figures very carefully and they will help you gain an edge in shaping your trading strategy in addition to using fundamental indicators as information about a country's economy.

Remember the value of a currency is also connected to national and international geopolitical events, elections, changes in government trade policies and political unrest or tension in a region which can all cause widespread instability in the financial markets. For example, when political tension escalated between Ukraine and Russia in 2016 the financial markets were hit hard, everything from commodities and Forex to equities.

The prices of sensitive commodities like oil and gas are an important fundamental indicator as high prices can hurt consumer spending and confidence and curtail the activities of certain businesses and of course government services on top of these important economic indicators.

The release of company results is a great trading opportunity for fundamental traders simply because the release date is usually well publicized beforehand and therefore reveals everything from the profitability and the health of the company to management's outlook and potential future dividend payments. Whilst not part of a company's earnings report, direct dealings can also cause wild swings in a company's share prices.

This is because investors often use them to determine whether directors are bullish or bearish about the firm. Make sure you stay up to date on upcoming scheduled economic data releases and news events and company announcements by watching country and international news week ahead keeps you in the know about the financial market.

## Technical Analysis

Technical analysis helps FOREX traders analyze price trends much like their counterparts in the equity market. The only difference is that FOREX markets are open 24 hours every day. In order to work with that 24 hour a day time frame, some types of technical analysis to be changed or modified. Technical Analysis is basically the framework in which forex traders study price movement.

The theory is that a person can look at historical price movements and determine the current trading conditions and potential price movement. Technical analysis relies on past price movement data to predict a currency pair's future value. Traders concentrate on charts of price movement and various analytical tools to assess a currency pair's strength or weakness.

In technical analysis, a trader scrutinizes the prices of specified currencies over time. In most cases, they will identify recurring patterns, which they then use to predict the movement of the market. Contrary to the Fundamental analysis that relies on computing current factors, or forecasting future factors, that are influencing a country's economy.

The following is a short list of technical analysis tools that are most commonly used in FOREX:
- Moving Averages
- Stochastic Oscillator
- Channel Breakout
- MACD (Moving Average Convergence Divergence)
- Candlestick charts
- Elliott Waves
- Fibonacci Studies
- Parabolic SAR
- Pivot Points

No discussion of technical analysis would be complete without an introduction to Forex chart basics.

**Bar Chart**

The very first Forex chart we will start with is called a "bar" chart. It gets its name because of its elongated bar-like shape. The typical bar on a bar chart is composed of 4 components:

**Open** – Opening price of the time period used
    **High** – Highest price of the time period used
    **Low**   – Lowest price of the time period used
    **Close** – Last price of the time period used
    Below is a typical bar of a bar chart

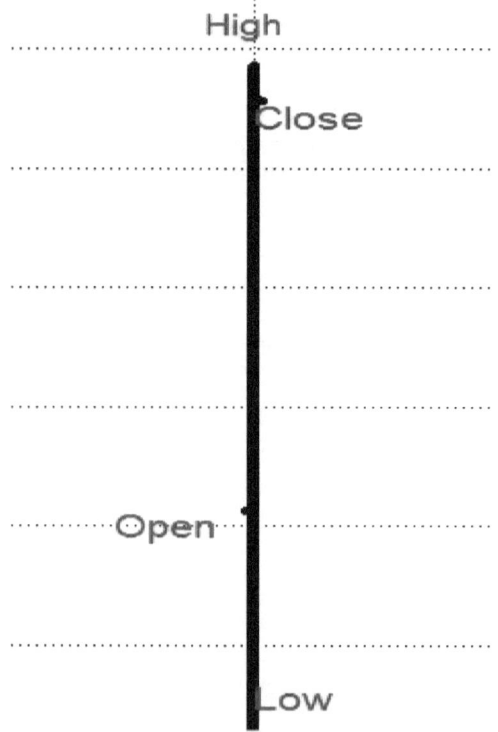

| Figure 1.1 Bar Chart |
| --- |

**Open** – Tick on left side of bar

**High** – Top of bar

**Low** – Bottom of bar

**Close** – Tick on Last price of the time period used

The chart below is a monthly chart of the EURUSD (Eurodollar/US Dollar) currency pair.

Monthly charts are longer-term charts used to get a feel for the "big picture" of the market. Many traders start here and then work their way through a series of smaller timeframe charts.

**Figure 1.2 Monthly EURUSD Data**

The weekly chart is the next timeframe available. The weekly chart confirms the EURUSD's upward movement since the beginning of 2009.

EURUSD - Weekly  FOREX  L=1.44204  0.00133  0.09%  B=1.44204  A=1.44224  O=1.44071  Hi=1.44466  Lo=1.43552  C=1.44204  ...

**Figure 1.3 Weekly EURUSD Data**

When we focus in on the daily chart, we see that the market continues to be in an uptrend.

Traders who are trend followers often take this "top down" approach to gain perspective on the market's movements and establish the direction of the trend. If a trader using this method feels that the upward trend will continue, they will see to find a suitable entry point for a long position in this market.

Figure 1.4 Daily EURUSD Data

Below is a very popular timeframe to use in Forex charting. It is a 4-hour bar chart. The 4-hour chart is an excellent chart to use in trading. It has become increasingly popular with those traders who feel that the smaller timeframes, i.e., 15-minute, 5 minutes, etc. move too erratically to base trading decisions on.

**Figure 1.5  4-Hour EURUSD Data**

The hourly chart is by far one of the most popular. It may be used by longer-term traders to refine their entries and exits. The 1-hour chart is also used by day traders who wish to gauge short-term market direction.

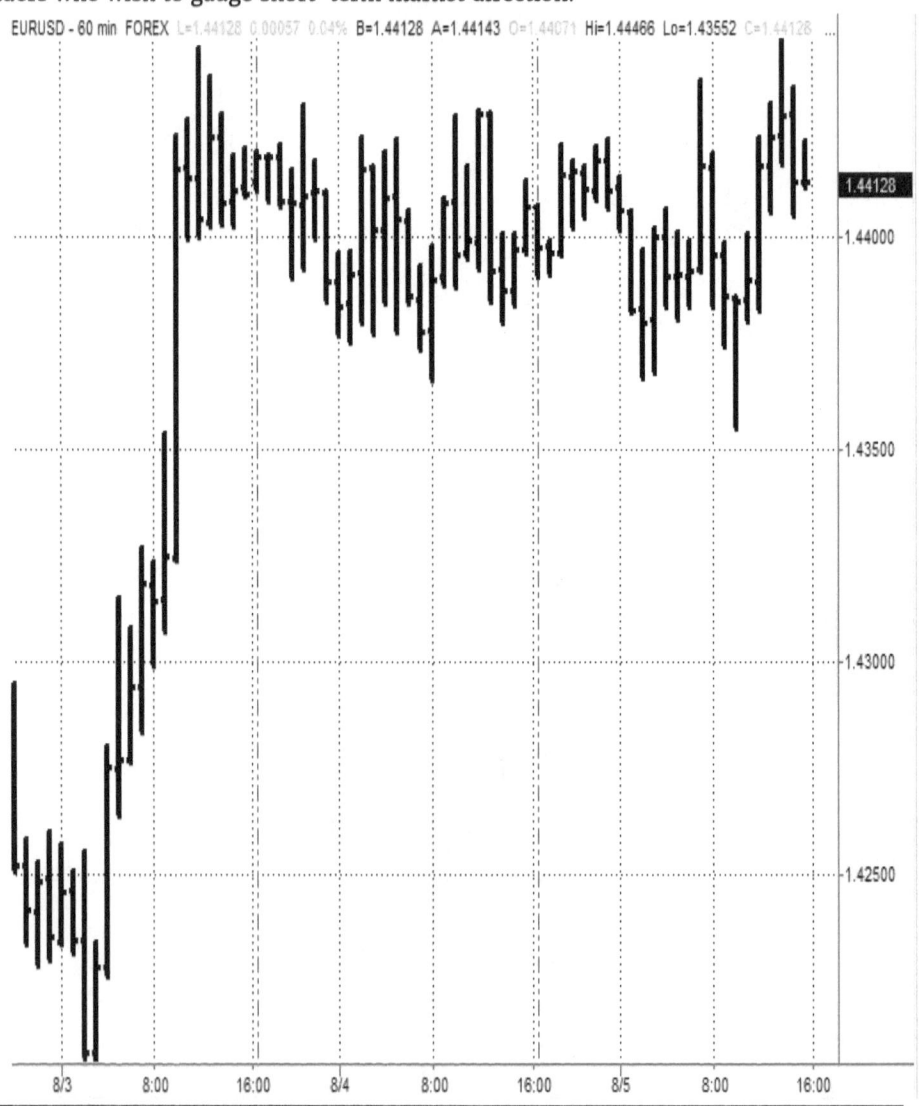

**Figure 1.6  1-Hour EURUSD Data**

The 5-minute chart is used almost exclusively by day traders.

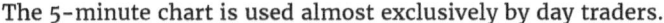

EURUSD - 5 min  FOREX  L=1.44138  0.00087  0.05%  B=1.44138  A=1.44156  O=1.44071  Hi=1.44466  Lo=1.43552  C=1.44138  V ...

**Figure 1.7 5-Minute EURUSD Data**

**Candlestick Chart**

Another form of Forex chart is the candlestick chart. Candlestick charting originated in Japan and is one of the oldest methods of charting in the world. Candlestick charting has enjoyed increased popularity and is now used by more Forex traders than ever.

EURUSD - Daily FOREX L=1.44107 0.00036 0.02% B=1.44107 A=1.44125 O=1.44071 Hi=1.44466 Lo=1.43552 C=1.44107 V ...

**Figure 1.8 Daily EURUSD Candlestick Data**

The name "candlesticks" comes from the appearance of the data on the chart. They price data looks like a "candle" with a "wick" on each end. In the chart above the solid green and solid red areas are known as the "real bodies". The gray lines that are extending from each end are known as "wicks". You may also hear "wicks" referred to as "shadows"

Candlesticks have become so popular because you can look at a candlestick chart and instantly get useful information. For instance, the green candles are called "bullish candles" because the price moved in an upward direction. The closing price for a green candle is always higher than the opening price. Red candles are called "bearish candles" because the price moved in a downward direction. The closing price for a red candle is always lower than the opening price.

The chart below shows a green candle at the start of a strong uptrend (see blue arrow).

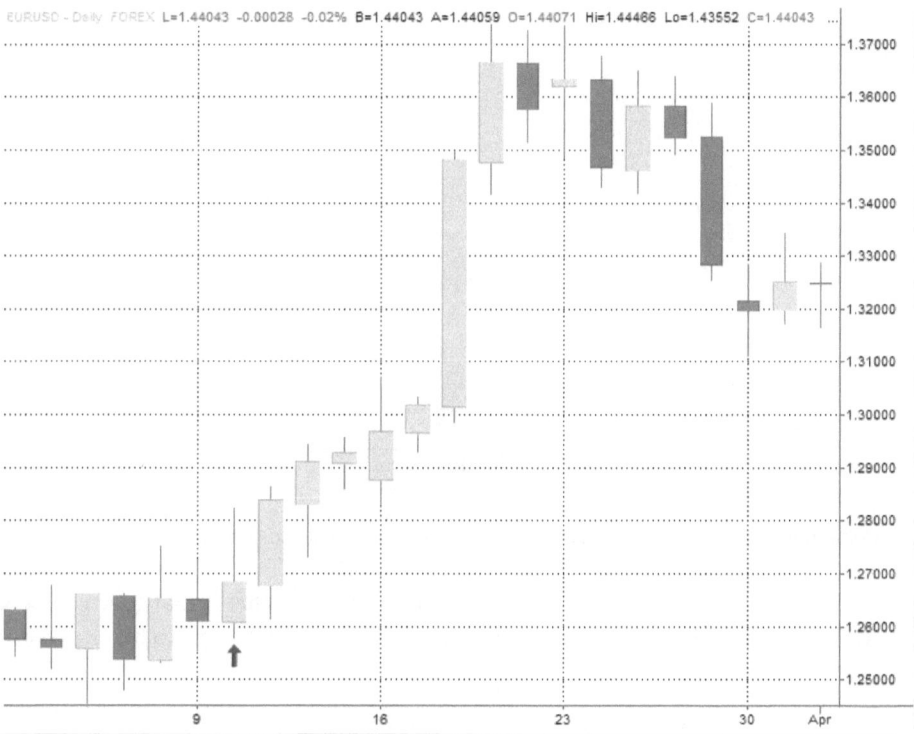

**Figure 1.9 Daily EURUSD Candlestick Data**

The chart below shows a red candle at the start of a strong downtrend (see red arrow).

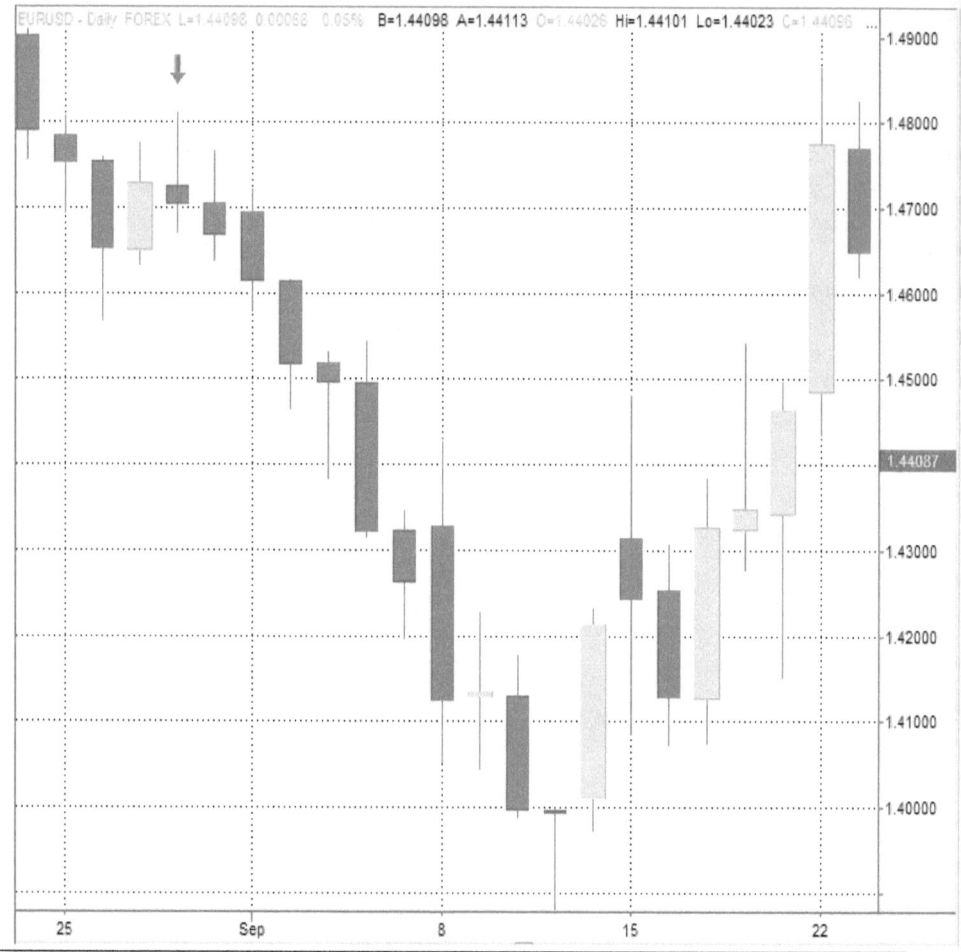

**Figure 1.10 Daily EURUSD Candlestick Data**

Consecutive candles of the same color generally indicate the continuation of a trend.

You can see from this brief introduction to candlestick charts that they can be very useful. After our brief introduction to candlestick charts it's time to move to our next topic.

Forex charts and technical indicators, also known simply as **"indicators"** have become a standard of Forex market analysis. An indicator is a visual element that is placed on the same Forex chart as the currency pair. It gets its name because it "indicates" something. An indicator can tell a trader when prices are at a favorable level to place a trade such as a buy trade or a sell trade.

**Figure 1.11 Daily EURUSD Data**

The green line we see below is an example of an indicator. This particular indicator is called a "**simple moving average**" or **SMA**. Arrows have been placed on the chart to represent buy and sell triggers. The "triggers" in this case are as follows:

When the price closes above the moving average then we have a buy trigger. When the price closes below the moving average we have a sell trigger.

**Figure 1.12 Daily EURUSD Data**

One question you may ask is, "When we see a trigger what do we do?" That's a good question. The standard way of using a moving average is to take the trade on the next bar after the trigger. This means that we would buy on the open of the bar "after" the trigger bar (blue up arrow bar in this case). The reverse is true of selling.

This is a simple example how you can use a simple Forex indicator to make a trading decision. Notice that this is just an observation and that in order to profit in Forex you will need to analyze the market further.

Why analyze a market? You need to analyze a market in order to make a decision to buy or sell...or do nothing at all. Let's further explore how Forex technical indicators can be used to help us make trading decisions. In fact, we are going to look at how technical indicators can be used to create simple Forex trading systems.

Simply put, a Forex trading system is a set of rules designed to help you trade Forex profitably. A Forex system generates trading signals. These trading signals tell the trader to take a certain action such as BUY or SELL.

The moving average we are using is a 9-period moving average. Since we are working with daily data, this we will be using a 9-day moving average.

| Date | Open | High | Low | Close | Avg. |
|------|------|------|-----|-------|------|
| 01/09/2008 15:59 | 1.47061 | 1.47422 | 1.46391 | 1.46583 | 1.46884 |
| 01/10/2008 15:59 | 1.46573 | 1.48129 | 1.46418 | 1.48033 | 1.47082 |
| 01/11/2008 15:59 | 1.48016 | 1.48189 | 1.47619 | 1.47740 | 1.47140 |
| 01/14/2008 15:59 | 1.47813 | 1.49141 | 1.47813 | 1.48680 | 1.47453 |
| 01/15/2008 15:59 | 1.48679 | 1.49209 | 1.47999 | 1.48033 | 1.47556 |
| 01/16/2008 15:59 | 1.48028 | 1.48590 | 1.45945 | 1.46515 | 1.47447 |
| 01/17/2008 15:59 | 1.46506 | 1.47145 | 1.45888 | 1.46410 | 1.47334 |
| 01/18/2008 15:59 | 1.46380 | 1.46946 | 1.46022 | 1.46212 | 1.47252 |
| 01/21/2008 15:59 | 1.46030 | 1.46040 | 1.44208 | 1.44543 | 1.46972 |
| 01/22/2008 15:59 | 1.44567 | 1.46435 | 1.43645 | 1.46285 | 1.46939 |

**Table 1.1 Daily EURUSD Raw Data with Simple Moving Average**

The table above shows the open, high, low, and close prices with the moving average values in green. As you can see the values of the moving averages changes as the prices of the EURUSD changes. It "moves" as the price moves, hence the name moving averages.

This particular moving average is calculated using the last 9 "closing" prices (listed under Close in the table).

Below is a daily EURUSD chart showing the buy and sell signals generated by using a simple 9-period moving average trading system we created.

**Figure 1.13 Daily EURUSD Data with Simple Moving Average**

One of the greatest advantages of using trading systems is to see how they would have performed on past data. If the results on past data look favorable then we may have a system that will work on future data as well. So how did our 9 period moving average system perform?

Let's take a look:

**Test Period: 1/20/2003–1/20/2008**
**Stop Loss Amount = $1000 (100pips)**

We have added a risk control measure in the form of a stop loss. A stop loss is an order designed to "stop loss" on a trading position. If the market moves in a way that causes your position to lose value the stop loss is designed to limit the amount of that loss.

10 Day Simple Moving Average System Net Profit = ~ – $2,300

So far this doesn't seem to be the type of moving average system that we would like to trade. Fortunately for us we can change the parameters of this indicator and research to find one which best suits our needs.

We have run a few tests and found the following:

42 Day Simple Moving Average System Net Profit = ~     $23,000

That's quite a difference in net profit isn't it? As you can see from this simple example it pays to do your research to find indicator settings that work well.

**Note:** The above examples and all examples that follow are for the purposes of illustration only. They are not meant to suggest that the displayed settings are to be used.

The next indicator we will explore is called the stochastic oscillator or stochastics for short. Unlike the simple moving average, the stochastic oscillator is not displayed on the same scale as the price. It is typically displayed below the prices as shown below.

The stochastic oscillator is grouped within type of technical indicators called oscillators because its value moves or oscillate between two extremes. These extremes range between 0–100.

**Figure 1.14 Daily EURUSD Data with 14-period Stochastic**

The typical interpretation of the stochastic oscillator is as follows:

- When the stochastic is over 80 that indicates that the market is overbought and losing upward momentum. Traders can either look to liquidate their long (buy) positions or look to sell.

- When the stochastic is below 20 that indicates that the market is oversold and losing downward momentum. Traders can either look to liquidate their short (sell) positions or look to buy.

**Figure 1.15 Daily EURUSD Data**

The above chart shows entries and exits based upon using a 14-day stochastic oscillator.

**Test Period: 1/20/2003–1/20/2008**
**Stop Loss Amount = $1000 (100pips)**

14 Day Stochastic Oscillator System Net Profit = ~ – $1,900

So far this doesn't seem to be the type of system that we would like to trade.

We have run a few tests and found the following:

6 Day and 46 Day Stochastic Oscillator System Net Profit = ~ $22,000

That's quite a difference in net profit isn't it? In this example you are shown two different parameters for the stochastic oscillator to introduce you to a new concept. In the first test we used a single parameter for both the buy and the sell trades. In the second test we used 6 days for our buy entries and 46 days for our sell entries.

Why does this seem to work so well? Because market may behave differently when moving downward than they do when moving upward so the best parameters for a bull (buy) market will not necessarily be the best parameters for a bear (sell) market.

**Note:** The above examples and all examples that follow are for the purposes of illustration only. They are not meant to suggest that the displayed settings are to be used.

You have probably heard about trading Forex without indicators. There is much being written about it these days, but it is actually nothing new. Trading without indicators is also called trading "price action". This means simply trading based upon the price itself and nothing else.

**Figure 1.16 Daily EURUSD Data**

What follows will be an example of trading without indicators. In the chart above you will see series of blue dots on prices bars and red dots on price bars. Although this is an example of trading without indicators the dots will help with the explanation. The blue dots represent when the high price has moved higher than the highest high of the previous 10 days. The red dots represent when a day's low price has moved lower than the lowest low of the previous 10 days. The red and blue arrows represent a sell (short) entry and a buy (long) entry respectively.

The chart below shows entries and exits based upon using a 10-day **breakout system**. The system is called a breakout system because the trade is taken when the price "breaks out" of a certain range. In this case we buy on a breakout of the highest high of the last 10 days and sell on a breakout of the lowest low of the last 10 days.

**Figure 1.17 Daily EURUSD Data**

**Test Period: 1/20/2003–1/20/2008**

**Stop Loss Amount = $1000 (100pips)**

14 Day and 8 Day Breakout System Net Profit = ~ $36,000

This is another system where we have used different parameters for the buy entry and the sell entry.

We have run a few tests and found the following:

22 Day and 8 Day Breakout System Net Profit = ~ $42,000

Once again, we see that testing different parameters pays off.

We have just gone over a few examples of how we can use a simple Forex chart with or without indicators to create a basic trading system. As we have stated before the parameters in the examples are not meant to be recommendations or suggestions for entering and exiting trades. They are here to illustrate the power that a few simple changes can have on a trading system's overall performance results.

**Determining Your Strategy** - It takes successful traders a while to develop and perfect the strategies that they use. Some prefer to use one particular study or formula while others use a variety of other strategies. Some experts would probably recommend that you try to find a good combination of both fundamental and technical analysis to make long-term predictions and to help you identify entry and exit points. Ultimately the decision is up to you.

It is also recommended that when you start in the FOREX market you should start by opening a demo account and paper trade as a way to practice making a profit on a regular basis.

Usually individuals who get into the FOREX market too quickly and without practicing to gain experience tend to lose money and ultimately aren't successful. So before investing your money into anything, it's always a good idea to get your feet wet before jumping in.

You will also have to learn to trade while keeping your emotions in check. It would be impossible to track the stop-loss points if you aren't able to execute them when you need to. It is highly recommended that you set your stop-loss and take-profit points to execute automatically and never change them unless it's a necessity.

Trust your decisions and stand by them or you will end up driving you and your broker crazy.

It's also important to follow the trends. Going against a trend is a pretty big gamble because statistically the FOREX market has tended to stick to trends so odds are you will be more successful if you don't go against the grain.

The FOREX market is the world's biggest market and people are drawn to it on a daily basis. But before you jump into the market, make sure you have a broker you trust and really put some effort into finding a strategy that will help you be successful.

## Chapter 8 - Forex Spread Basics

Forex is the trading between two different forms of currencies. Those two currencies make up the pricing of Forex paired as Currency1/Currency2. When trading, you have to sell one currency in order to purchase the other currency. To exit this trade, the reverse must be performed.

Take the following example, you think the Japanese Yen is going to rise in value compared to the US Dollar and want to cash in on the growth rate. In a Forex trade, you sell US Dollars in order to purchase Japanese Yen. To exit the trade, you sell the Japanese Yen back and purchase US Dollars. The goal of this trade is to buy more US Dollars back than when you sold them, meaning the USD/JPY exchange rate has risen and you made a profit.

The trouble today with these trades is the deceiving marketing to traders that almost all Forex brokers use. The brokers claim to have the tightest spreads in the industry. Spreads in the Forex spot market are a complicated, hard to understand topic, but one of the greatest factors in your trading profitability. It is important to understand this topic to unlock the best Forex trade gains.

A spread is defined as the difference between the price you buy at, known as the ask price, and the price you sell at, known as the bid price. The spread is measured in pips. For example, if a EUR/USD (Euro/US Dollar) quote is 1.2222/4, then the spread would be 2 pips or if a EUR/USD (Euro/US Dollar) quote is 1.22225/40, then the spread would be 1.5 pips.

A .5 pip spread drop doesn't seem like a large difference, but it can actually mean the difference between a loss pip spread and a gain pip spread.

Wide spreads result in higher asking prices, meaning you pay more when you buy, and lower bidding prices, meaning you get less when you sell leading to a loss on your part and a gain by the broker. This is where brokers get their money and makes it harder for you to make gains. However, Forex brokers don't usually earn the full spread using this method, most lose gains when they hedge client positions. This spread is helpful in compensating the market maker from the time of your trade to when the broker's net exposure is hedged. The Forex broker's net exposure when hedged could be an entirely different value.

These spreads will affect the return on your trading strategy and should be taken into great consideration when trading. Your interest as a Forex trader is to ask low and bid high, similar to stock trading but contrary to the nature of wide spreads.

Therefore, you would want to wait for a half-pip lower spread as it can easily turn your non profitable trade into a high gaining trade.

Although tighter spreads translate to "things are good for you", it doesn't mean anything profit wise without following through. If for instance you see a tight spread, but your trade gets mixed with a few wide pips or is rejected altogether, you won't actually receive the tight spread. Repeated occurrence of this would mean your broker is using some tricks to stop tight spreads.

Some tricks brokers use include: rejected trades, delayed execution, slipping, and stop-hunting all help to stop acquiring tight spreads. Repeated offense means your broker is showing tight spreads, but switching for wider ones.

Comparing brokers is a fairly hard task to do since spread policies between each differ greatly and are difficult to understand. For example, some brokers give you the choice of a fixed spread that remains the same no matter the state of the market. This seems like a good deal, but fixed spreads are usually higher than variable ones. In short, this option is like paying insurance on your trade.

Another example, some brokers conversely use varying spreads that are dependent of the market state. If the market is in good condition, the spreads will be tight, but as soon as the market worsens, the spread will begin to widen. Fixed and variable rates both have pros and cons, but the better one to choose ultimately depends are your trading style. Either rate you chose relies on your quality of execution.

Brokers also use different spreads based on the individual's account. A client that has a large account will receive a tighter spread. A client that makes larger trades will receive a tighter spread. A client referred by another broker will actually receive a wider spread so the company can cover the cost of referral.

These policies differ from broker to broker, some offer the same spreads to everyone. Some brokers use different deceiving tactics and make it hard to uncover the truth about a company's spread policy.

Be wary when talking with brokers and never trust the promises you hear. A lot of traders take the broker's word on these promises, resulting in some serious loss. Try out various brokers before settling or ask an expert who have tried many different brokers, it always pays to do your homework.

## Chapter 9 – Tips For Trading Forex Successfully

Indisputably, trading involves much more than just what is confined in some short tips. A solid trading system is necessary, supported by experience, a courageous spirit, and, of course, capital. But, for most people just starting in trading, and others who are possibly losing their enthusiasm and self-confidence due to large, but hopefully temporary, drops in market values, a basic overview can restore clarity and certainty to your trading. With that goal in mind, some tips are presented that we hope will assist you as you seek to navigate these exciting financial waters.

1. If a position is showing negative activity, do not increase the risk by getting in deeper.
This is the same as the old trader's saying, "Never add to a losing trade".

2. Never fail to decide upon a stop and a profit objective prior to your entering a trade. Use your knowledge of the market to determine placement of stops, not the amount of money you have available in your account. It is not feasible to conduct the trade if an adequate stop is too costly.

3. Keep in mind the privilege of a position. A market judgment should not be made when you are already a position. Once you are in a position all of your decisions about adding to the position, protecting the position, or exiting the position should already be made.

4. Sometimes circumstances change and when you determine that, you make the choice to exit a trade. Don't assume you can just take your choice of price with the easy plan to exit at the market. One example of this is when some surprise big news comes out following a big event. This can push the acceptable level of volatility beyond that which works with your trading methods.

5. Don't buy a dull market in a Bear market and don't sell a dull market in a Bull market.

Simply translated this means that if there is no momentum in one direction or the other then the chance of the follow through necessary to profit is slim. Enter trades that you have determined will have the greatest chance for success.

6. When the market is very volatile or is experiencing a lack of liquidity, you should not trade at all. Even when there is potential for extreme volatility caution should be exercised. Although volatile market movements hold the potential for huge gains, they can be far too unpredictable. Always avoid unnecessary risk when trading.

7. It is important to keep in mind that the same trading systems do not always work in both up and down markets. If you have a trend-following Forex trading system you must understand that there is always the potential for it to perform less than admirably in sideways markets.

8. You need to adjust your trading strategy with each market type: up trending, range bound, and down trading. Ideally with a trend-following trading system it would be best to avoid sideways markets altogether. There is nothing wrong with a trend-following system which "stands aside" during sideways markets...in fact it is preferred that it stand aside.

9. Choose trades that move along with the dominant market pattern. Although up market and down market patterns are always discernable, one or the other is always the most dominant. For instance, during an up market, sell signals are repeatedly taken, only to be respectively stopped.

This all goes back to the timeless statement, "The trend is your friend". Trading in the direction with the greatest probably for success is just common sense. This is not to say that you can't develop a counter-trend trading system that can be profitable.

10. A sell signal is just a failed buy signal; a buy signal is just a failed sell signal.

11. A losing trade is always much less difficult to enter!

13. Follow your gut instincts; if you don't feel good about something, don't trade.

14. When you hear a Forex trading tip ignore it. Go with what you know and that is the trading system you have taken the time to develop faith in.

15. Current events in the news only are significant when they DO NOT propel the market in the direction of the news.

16. You gain a degree of understanding when you read yesterday's paper today, armed with knowledge of the market's activity today. You realize that yesterday's market activity has no impact on today's.

17. Never make your trade decisions based on the direction of a gap. The market should not force you into a trade.

18. Use the rule of "in late, out early," being mindful that the first tick and the last tick are by far the most expensive.

19. Exit when you realize everyone else is in.

20. Don't add to the risk factor by trading when ill. Trading can be strenuous enough without the added stress of not feeling well. Avoid trading when there is anything which might affect your trading discipline.

21. Your unit of trading should only be altered when you have a plan of attained goals. You should establish a reduction plan for times when the market experiences lower volume or your trading is a little off.

A good money management system is part of every good trading plan. It will reduce your position size when your trading system gets out of sync with the market and increase your position size when your trading system is in sync with the market.

22. Don't be cocky or boastful in any way. Enjoy your trading success with pride and modesty.

23. Judge your success by the growth of your equity over time and not by the success of individual trades. Even a bad trader can have a winning streak.

24. Taking a break from trading for a day will often break a losing streak.

25. If you are on a roll, keep going! You are doing something right. Why in the world would you want to stop? When you and your trading methods are in sync with the markets just keep your winning streak going.

26. When you are having an off day, turn off the computer screen and find something else to do. Don't just keep at it when you are losing; that doesn't make any sense.

Walking away for a while is not an easy thing to do, but it is important to discipline yourself to do it.

27. Scalpers reduce the number of variables affecting market risk by being in trades or positions only for a few seconds. Day traders reduce market risk by being in trades for minutes.

It makes perfect sense that the smaller your profit target the quicker it will be hit. This is what has attracted so many to day trading. If this style of trading interests you please keep in mind the following:

**Increased Frequency Of Trading = Increased Transactions Costs**

28. The decision to convert a scalp or day trade into a position trade means that you did not understand the risks of the trade adequately.

29. Don't let an opportunity that you missed trouble you. Opportunities are around every bend.

There are new opportunities every single day. So many new traders like to talk about the big money that they left on the table. Experienced traders are happy to have taken their slice of the price action. Rarely, if ever will you get 100% of the possible potential profit of ANY trade.

30. You are better served by learning to trade Forex than searching for an elusive secret formula.

31. Don't trust the advice of others because they probably didn't do as much research as you did.

This is a statement that really hits home. It does sometime seem that the grass is greener on the other side of the fence. There will be days when it seems like everyone else is in the know except you. Don't let that bother you. If you've done your homework your time will come.

32. Mentally establish the reality of what is happening, good or bad, up or down, by affirming it aloud amid a mind full of preconceived notions.

If you have a losing trade don't be afraid to say to yourself, "Cleary my trading method did not work out on that trade, but my research has shown me that if I continue on this path I will succeed!"

33. Flexibility is absolutely necessary to be a success at day trading. You need to be an informed participant, understanding the market potential for both sides of the market. An informed decision-maker makes trades with understanding of what is the current market climate.

34. Deliberate, even bemoan and confess your errors in discipline. You will continue to make these types of errors for many years, it seems, and so reminding yourself may delay the inevitable.

35. If this list made you uncomfortable, then you are like many other traders in two ways:

A. You have enough trading experience to understand that the mistakes are yours, not the market's, and you seek to overcome these inadequacies.

B. Oddly enough, you have become one with the market. You could not leave, and you do not want to. Wherever you go in life, you will ALWAYS keep tabs on the market.

# Chapter 10 – Further Market Wisdom To Help You Trade Successfully

1. Trade in the direction of the trend with small accounts under $25,000. Forex trading permits bi-directional trading which appeals to beginners, but your odds are better trading in the direction of the trend in the long term.

2. Keep two accounts: one is a real one and one is a demo. Use the demo account to test alternative trades, continuing with lifelong learning, although an active trader.

3. Stop trying to predict the future; you can't. There are no leading indicators. There is software on the market to predict market trends, but if you think about it, if it worked, would they tell you about it?

This is extremely important to understand. By the time you search out and think you have found the Holy grail of Forex trading you could have amassed a fortune in profits.

4. Use the daily charts to help you time your trades: the four-hour charts and one hour charts. Trading at 15 and 30 minute increments takes quite a lot of skill.

5. Be an observer of patterns. Trade the pattern instead of the time frame. You will see hesitation, reversal and breakout patterns quite often.

6. The more lots you trade, the safer, if you can afford it. Trading consists of technical analysis, money management and a lot of emotional energy. It is difficult to make the best entry and exit decisions with just one lot alone. This is because you don't have the flexibility to take partial profits or add to your position.

7. Trading at the extremes seems to up the odds that you are going in the right direction. Extreme trading is actually conservative trading!

8. Carefully review the major currency pair before taking a position in any of them. You may have missed something.

**They are:**

**USDJPY – US dollar/Yen**
**EURUSD – Euro/US dollar**
**USDCHF – US dollar/Swiss**
**GBPUSD – Pound/US dollar**

(see chart of these below)

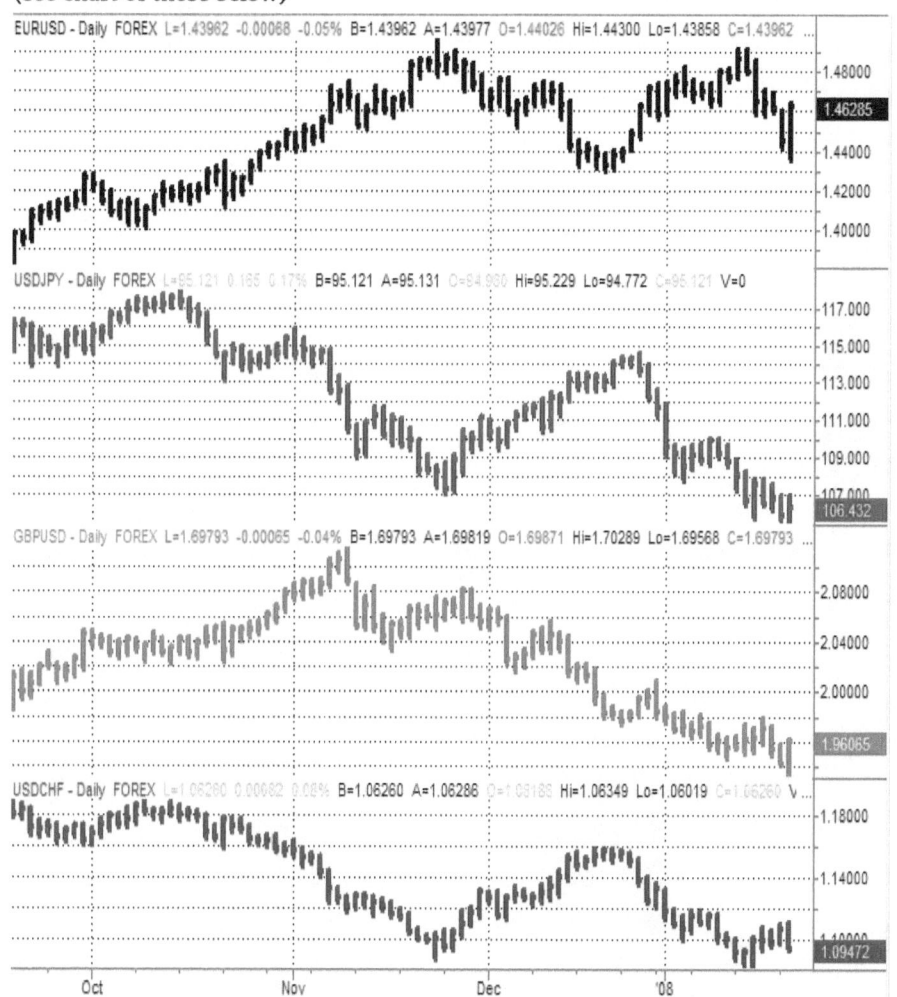

**Figure1.0 Major Currency Pairs – Daily Data**

9. There is something called the "Upside Down rule." It sounds silly, but works. If you can turn a chart upside down and it does not look any different to you, then stay away from it.

These are some of the important rules you should never break when trading. Applying these rules consistently with an adequate amount of discipline can lead to being a profitable trader. These rules can exponentially improve your success if understood, implemented and practiced consistently.

Setting up and Implementing specific goals and objectives - Important to your success is having specific goals and objectives.

It is amazing how often we meet our objectives, and reach our goals when we speak aloud and write them down. To be successful your objectives must be achievable and measurable. Making money is the first objective when trading; but shouldn't keep you from having objectives not strictly related to cash.

Reward and risk go together, without planning and being prepared for high risk (draw-downs) you can't expect to see high returns. Your goals and objectives must be geared toward you and must contain these characteristics if they are going to be useful:

• They must be measurable regarding completion and the timeframe involved

• They need to be realistic and achievable

• They must be worth the time and effort put into them

• They need to be positive - As an example, here are some actual objectives (bearing in mind this is only a partial list):

• Create 2 new positive-expectancy trading systems yearly

• Make fewer errors implementing your trading systems yearly

• Take 2 weeks' vacation yearly

Note, only one example is about making money, it has a measurable objective similar to a draw-down. It is not guaranteed.

Knowing what you are trying to gain and trying to achieve will make your objectives more obtainable. It will help you to pay attention to what you want to achieve and to effectively gauge your trading strategy's progress and success.

**Consistency and discipline** - To obtain the full potential of your trading system you will need to take every trading entry, adjust every stop and close out every trade when your trading system directs you to. Extreme confidence in your trading system, quality technology, and the discipline to stick to your plan are necessary for success. Having and underlying belief about consistency and discipline allows you to have a plan for all situations and helps define consistency.

Your trading plan must include these items to be successful:

• Complete rules for entering, adding to, and getting out of your positions

• How to respond should your trading tools become inoperable.

• What to do if you are unable to trade

• What to do if you lose a defined percentage of your account

• What to do if the markets are closed leaving you in your current positions

Without these answers consistency and discipline cannot be obtained and the reasons for monetary loss cannot be determined.

**Let your profits run** - When you have a profitable trade the fear of losing unrealized cash will cause you to want to quit while you are ahead. Most trading consists of small winners and losers over a long time, with a few big winners. This is what makes the difference between profitability, breaking even or losing. Your ability to let big winners happen determines your yearly performance. The key is to have trailing stops outside the noise of the market so they don't get stopped out during the normal trading process. Prepare yourself to give up a large portion of a trade's open profit makes this difficult to implement.

Adding to a winner and widening your stops (do not widen your stops if you are already in a trade) helps you capture the largest amount of profit. Your trade has shown itself to be a winner, the risk is low, add to the position rather than implement stops that are too tight.

It is imperative that your rules are pre-defined allowing for large winning trades.

**Cut your losses short** - This rule is as difficult as the one above. Just as profitability comes from big wins, preserving your capital comes from avoiding the big losers.

Setting a maximum loss point allows you to know how much is being risked on this position. Your exit price tells you a trade is a loser and when to exit. 100% accuracy in regards to our maximum loss is unobtainable due to gaps at the open and because of limit moves in futures. Having these rules and keeping them saves us from catastrophic loses when we have a series of trades that keep going against our position.

A losing position at your maximum loss point means get out right away. Trades are either winners or losers. The chances of a losing trade turning around are absolutely unknown to any of us. Accept the loss, move on. Financially and mentally you will be in a much better place. Even if this loser turned around, the stress and bad feelings from holding your position are not worth it.

**Never add to a losing trade** - If a trade shows itself to be a winner add to it then, but not before. In many cases your trade will hit your stop loss, not changing directions. Sometimes a trade turns around before hitting your stop loss and sometimes after doing so, regardless it is never worth it adding to a loser.

**Don't take too much risk** - Risking too much capital on a single trade is a devastating mistake. Losing all your capital puts you out of the game and prevents you from continuing. Risking all of your account on one loser will put you out of the game.

You should only risk 1-3% of your available capital on any individual trade. This is calculated using the size and difference between the entry price and your maximum stop price in regards to the amount of capital allocated to the system. With these combined it is almost certain that you will not hit your maximum draw-down for the year or lose your trading capital. If you worry about the size of a trade it is too big, use a lower amount. Longevity in any trading market is the key to making money. Trade slowly over a long time with a minimum amount of risk.

**Only trade Forex trading systems with a positive mathematical expectation** - That's a fancy way of saying that a positive expectancy trading system determines how much money you will make in a year based on your number of trades, amount of capital allocated to the system and the accuracy in using your trading signals. If you don't know if your trading system is positive expectancy then you shouldn't be trading.

Expectancy is calculated using profit or loss on each trade; dividing it by initial risk, and taking the average of this number over a series of trades. Successful traders trade systems when the odds are in their favor.

You will want to minimize all of you trading business costs. Some trading systems only offer marginal profitability due to trading implementation costs which can be the difference between profit and loss. Modern electronic brokers as well as fully automated trade processing and execution make it worthwhile to look for a low-cost implementation of a trading system.

Choosing the right broker can significantly reduce high commissions, wide spreads and large amounts of slippage leading to a systems usability or lack thereof.

**Educate yourself** - Competing at the highest level in the trading business requires you to be well-educated about what you are doing. This will help you to become an expert in your trading business.

**Avoid trading scared money** - Needing to make a certain amount of money per month to avoid being in financial trouble is the quickest way to mess up your trading discipline, rules, objectives, and profits. Trade with a reasonable amount of risk used to achieve a good reward. Never trade if you need the money to pay bills. Never trade if your business and personal expenses are not covered by another form of income. This is how hasty decisions get made.

## Chapter 12 - Forex Mindset

The average person has a very simple life, because of this they are blissfully unaware of exactly what the problems are that they can encounter. Knowing what the potential disasters are before you get started can help you to ensure you do not find yourself in the same situation. Remember, there is nothing wrong with learning from the mistakes of others and a bit of effort carefully placed into the proper research will allow you to reduce your expenses, save hassle and make money much faster.

The very first mistake that is made is not entering a stop loss order. This is a useful tool that will allow you to quickly and easily set a minimum to the currency that you hold. Once it drops to a certain level it would be arranged to automatically sell. The benefit of this is you do not even have to watch the market directly to have your currency sell at the level that you desire.

This is quite useful in the event that you are not interested in taking a loss on your transactions. Because of the turbulence that the market gives, it is very dangerous to not have a stop loss order in at almost all times.

Allowing yourself to become wrapped up in emotion as well will cost you thousands of dollars in the Forex market. Knowing that you have some problems with emotion will allow you to learn how to distance yourself while still getting all of the benefits that you need.

If you start to think that you are never going to have any problems with disasters striking you will quickly discover just how hard it can be to make things work out properly. Taking some time to practice separating yourself from the situation is extremely important.

Another critical mistake that is often made is trying to predict what the market is going to do. This can create some serious problems because it can often lead to overconfidence. You absolutely have to stick to just facts rather than trying to just guess or predict what the market will do. If you decide to try guessing you might luck out and make a correct guess or two, but the majority of the times you attempt at just guessing you are going to lose money.

Avoid this situation if at all possible and instead focus on getting all of the information you can possibly gather together to avoid making an incorrect decision.

One of the other mistakes that is often made is treating investing as if it is a hobby. This creates a lot of problems for people when they are trying to work on straightening out details.

Making money at Forex trading is possible, but only if you treat it like an actual business. In order to be truly successful, you need a business mindset and you need to be thinking clearly when you are working on all of the transactions. If you have no clue what you are doing, you will quickly discover that the entire process is useless and provides you no major benefits. In order to really enjoy the process, you absolutely must take the time to determine your goals and a course of action. Diving right in and getting started working is not a safe idea, not is it a wise investment of your money.

The correct mindset is one of the biggest things that is required in order to be secure while engaging in transactions in Forex. Knowing what the major problems tend to be and working diligently to avoid them will help you to ensure you get on track properly and stay there.

Taking control of your Forex experience really is possible but you absolutely must ensure you get started successfully. Starting out properly is much easier than trying to fix your mistakes after the fact. Success is possible, but avoiding these mistakes will help further ensure all of your success.

## Chapter 13 – Forex Secrets

For most people there are plenty of confusing ideas about exactly what Forex is, and how it can benefit you. Trying to clear up these problems is extremely important and can help you to ensure that you get started on the right foot.

What is Forex?

In simple terms, Forex is the foreign exchange market that allows investors to meet together for the common purpose of buying and selling currency. Using this market people from all around the world are able to quickly buy and sell currency regardless of the time of day. The market allows for transactions that are both large in size, and also those that are significantly smaller as well.

When is Forex open?

This is the great news for most investors. The Forex market is actually open 5 days a week, 24 hours a day. You might think that this is really strange, but if you consider that Forex is a global market place where people from all around the world are coming together to buy and sell currency it is really easy to see how the market can actually operate near continuously without having to close. The market does close for a very brief period of time during the weekend though, but as soon as the first time zone changes to Monday morning the market is open yet again.

Can I really trade at any time of day?

Yes, this is why the Forex market is so popular. While the stock market is only open a few short hours each week, the Forex market is open almost continuously. This allows people with a wide variety of schedules to all come together for the purpose of buying and selling the currency. In order to really get the best results, it is important to work at a time when you are free to think and for some people this might be 3 a.m. and for others it might be closer to 10a.m. Having the flexibility to submit transactions at a time that is best for you will allow you faster results, and a better idea of how the market really works.

Are there any minimums?

This is something that tends to be set by the brokers themselves. If you are concerned about the minimum amounts, you should always talk to the brokers that you are considering to find someone who will fit your budget and needs. Taking a gamble on a larger minimum than you can reasonably afford might create disaster so knowing that you can reasonably afford the minimum is critical. If the minimum that you are told at first is not suitable, you can always feel free to look for a different broker who can fit all of your needs.

Do I have to go somewhere to trade?

This is one of the best aspects of the Forex market, because it occurs online there is no reason at all to worry about having to get out of your house and go to the market. You can simply locate the nearest computer to take care of most of your transactions. This allows you to quickly and easily get things in order no matter where you are. Because of the flexibility, you can even stay up to date on how the market is moving while you are on vacation without the hassle that you might imagine.

The Forex market represents a place where everyone is able to meet together for a variety of transactions that can occur quickly. Using the market carefully it is possible to find a lot of success. It is extremely important though that you take the time to carefully review all of your options before you get started to ensure you have the best success possible. Small amounts of effort in the beginning will help you to ensure you are successful without having to spend years going to school to study financial topics.

With the Forex market capturing the attention of people all around the world it is very important that you learn a few key tips to help you ensure that you are properly on your way towards getting the results that you are after. Simply jumping into the market is not likely to give you the results desired and instead will leave you frustrated. Following these three simple tips will help you to ensure you get the best results possible from all of your Forex transactions.

1. Stick to pairs – This is a golden rule of thumb. While of course you can trade the currencies across each other without penalty, it is a wise idea to limit the currencies that you deal with. Even better to restrict them to pairs that you can easily compare to each other. Of course, you can compare the USD to all of the other currencies if you are looking to engage in a new transaction, but if you are considering all of the currency choices available it might take you hours to pick one which could still turn wrong. It is much better instead to choose a pair that you always use together. For example, you could do pairs involving the USD and the GBP with another pair consisting of CAD and AUD. By always trading within these pairs, you are going to significantly decrease the amount of information you need to review for each trade.

2.     Never make a trade without research – This should be an easy tip to follow. If you are a new investor, this is extremely important because it will help you to learn the market, if you are a seasoned investor it will help you to keep from becoming overconfident.  Decisions in the market should never be made unless you are basing them on actual proper research.  Simply using a gut feeling is not acceptable and will result in losses.  Taking a couple of minutes for some quick research is not that difficult and if you are trading in pairs as mentioned in the previous tip you will find that it is quite easy and fast to do.

3.     Plan your strategy out – If you were going to build a house and expect it to stand you would do plenty of research to get ready then you would spend a bit of time trying to ensure that you have all of the materials, knowledge and people necessary to be successful.  This is a strategy for building a house and in a similar manner; you need a strategy for Forex.  Diving in is never a good idea for anything and Forex is certainly not any different.  Finding true success means having a specific goal in mind, what do you really want from the market?  Are you looking to buy a car?  Are you looking to fund your retirement?  Are you even looking to become the richest person in the world?  You need to know where you are trying to go so that you can set up a strategy that you stick to without fail.

While Forex might look impossible to succeed with, following these three simple tips will help you to find the success that you are looking for without leaving your anxious or stressed.  A few minutes following each tip when you first start trading will save a lot of hassle, and for those already trading a review to ensure you follow these suggestions will help you to improve your overall experience.

## Chapter 14 – How To Buy Foreign Exchange Currency?

Many people get started in the Forex market without using a broker and are quite happy, however, there are plenty of others who do use a broker and there are some great reasons. The Forex market can be extremely complicated and complex. Having someone to help you ensure you make the correct decisions is a good way to help reduce your mistakes when you first get started in the Forex market. The benefits of a broker will typically far outweigh the actual expense of a broker that you have to pay as well.

A good Forex broker will be able to help you in regards to learning how to obtain accurate real time quotes. The important consideration here is that because the quotes are real time, they will continuously change. You cannot typically get the same quote several times simply because people are always trading. Due to this having an accurate quote is helpful, but it is just that a quote which can still change. Still yet though, basing decisions off of these quotes is very important and can allow you to accurately ensure that you are moving in the right direction.

Look for a Forex broker who will manage your account for you if you do not have the time to manage it yourself. This is something that is opted for quite often for people who have overly busy schedules and can be arranged easily. The fees that you will pay under this arrangement are typically higher, but you can still come out ahead if you choose an experienced broker. It is important that you ask for information on the brokers returns though before handing over your money. You need to be able to see just how successful they are with the money that they are investing.

A Forex broker should also be able to help you with deciding what to buy and what to sell. Because of the experience that they have, they can generally look at the market newsfeeds and quickly determine the best transaction to make. This is a skill that you too will acquire with time, but especially in the beginning the advice of a broker can significantly speed up the research process.

A great Forex broker should also be able to recommend a good Forex trading software for you to use. Many different software packages exist, and many are better than others are. Trying to decipher which software packages are truly the best is not always simple. Having someone who can actually recommend a good package that will allow you the information; you need, without overwhelming you is a very important consideration. It is also vital that you have a software package that works with your computer and investors who are using computers that do not run Windows operating systems are often at a disadvantage. A Forex broker can point you towards suitable software regardless of the operating system that you use.

While the expense of a Forex broker might seem quite large, they are extremely useful for the beginning investor. Trying to ensure that you are able to really decipher the market can be difficult and using a good broker will make things so much easier on you. Taking the time to carefully study all of your options allows you to be absolutely certain that you do not select the wrong broker.

## Chapter 15 – Making Foreign Exchange Money

With so many different theories abounding about how to make money, it is no wonder that a lot of people are quite confused about how to get started and succeed. In order to really make some serious money you need to take a few things into consideration and always keep this at the front of your mind. Remember, you should never make any transactions in the Forex market without thinking and these small thoughts will be very helpful for you as you move onto some of the more advanced options as well.

Your first goal is taking the time and effort to really determine how much you want to make. Once you have determined this it should be rather obvious that these three suggestions will help you significantly. Using them in all of your transactions can help you a lot, but these are only a beginning basis for suggestions and should never be considered an all-inclusive solution to your needs.

The first thing to remember and practice is that you really need to work with more than short term trades. You should not do this because it will increase your fees and often decrease your profit margin. You are essentially burning money when you do this, which is doing you and your finances absolutely no good.

In order to be truly beneficial in the system you have to be willing to take the effort to watch the market to see exactly how long you can keep your money invested. Making short-term investments might have your money back to you faster, but it will also have a significantly lower profit level as well.

The second thing is that you should also consider increasing the amount that you invest each time. The general rule of thumb is to never invest more than 1-3% of your total account. This is great, especially if you have a very large account, but what happens if you only have a few thousand in there? Assuming you have $10,000 in your account and only invest 3%, you have just made a measly $300. This is certainly not worth the risk, time nor hassle that is involved. Instead, you could make thousands in returns if you invested wiser.

The final tip that will help you significantly as well is to always avoid working with transactions that would require you to have additional transactions out at the same time. If you cannot get all of your details worked out properly, you will find that it is very difficult to work out. Taking a bit of time to ensure you get all of your details line from one transaction is best before you start the next. Because of this, you need to consider going to the effort of only doing a single transaction each time. This might require more time to build up profits, but you will not confuse yourself and make a terrible decision.

Clear thinking will help you a lot, but knowing when to buck the standard rules is very important as well. Going the proper direction will help you to be as successful as possible, while still getting the experience you need on your own without having to use an expensive broker who manages all of your transactions for you. Forex is not impossible to learn, but you can quickly discover why so many people have significant issues in the market once you start looking at all of the ways that mistakes can really be made.

## Chapter 16 – Researching Your Trades

If you have ever done any research into Forex, you have no doubt heard a lot of different stories. These are all truths and realities that have to be considered and analyzed to the best of your ability but there are plenty of myths floating around as well. In order to help you get started as quickly and easily as possible, you should take a bit of time to really review and study all of your options and choices as well as learn what is really going on within the Forex market.

You first realization is that success rests firmly upon your own hands. If you do not have any success, it will be your own fault. Even if you work with a broker who makes trades for you, the failure is all yours. The success is all yours as well but of course comes across much nicer than a failure. Most people look for someone else to make responsible when things go wrong, but this is just not how it works.

You should also be very careful to realize that not everyone is going to be advanced in the markets. Some people have great difficulty coming up with the way that the market works. This is normal and tends to happen, especially in the beginning because of all of the choices that are offered. You need to ensure that you are keeping your options open but still remember that all of those options are a bit complicated and certainly none of them are easy.

You need to also do your research before you start trading. This will help you to form the correct opinions about each potential transaction. Not all investors are created equally and because of this there are some who will constantly run around freaking out over each small change and there are others who are very laid back. Most newcomers tend to be worried, which is something that will likely happen regardless of what you say or do before that first trade.

Use the technical tools that are available. Any charts, graphs and other materials should be closely studied before you take the time to get started on your investment to ensure that they are accurate and offer all of the best information. If the information is incorrect it will do you no good to take that information to use for the basis of your trades. You need information that is correct without having to sell a kidney to receive it.

Selecting a good broker is also important when you are getting started. As an investor, you might not know anything about the Forex market initially and will require someone who is smart to help you set it up. This is where a broker comes into play; they are reasonably priced and great at helping to answer all of the questions that you might have in regards to the Forex market.

Always feel free to shoot the broker you select a quick message. You have the ability to use their experience to your benefit and this is going to be a huge help as you are attempting to get started investing in Forex all on your own. Careful selection of brokers is important but certainly not impossible, so take your time to select the right broker for all of your needs.

# Chapter 17 – Taking Loses In FX Trading

There are a lot of situations that can make financial tools turn quite dangerous the average consumer has not a clue in the least what they are doing and this all equals out to a bundle of problems for most people. If you find yourself in this position where you are messing around with the Forex market, it is very important that you carefully consider each of your options. For the average consumer there are far too many mistakes that can be made. Choosing incorrectly will quickly find you losing all of your money instead of getting further ahead with things as you want.

Taking just the smallest amount of time to study is always very important, but typically, most consumers just do not take this time. Rather they are busy worrying about ways in which they can strike it rich fast and for the most part the Forex market is not the place for that type of thinking. It is extremely important it is extremely important to take proper considerations and care before making any decision regarding Forex transactions as people make the mistake of rushing right in which you create enormous headaches in the near future.

The Forex market is extremely dangerous for anyone who does not know what they are doing. To get started it is quite easy to learn how to make wise decisions in the market though with careful consideration and planning you can be up and running in a matter of days though, it is very important that you consider that the wrong transaction could quickly enter your Forex career. Taking a plunge and just getting started in the market with no time to really review what you are doing or could potentially do can quickly cause you a serious financial problem.

In order to really engage in safe transactions in the market it is very important that you take some time to read up on how the market operates and also exactly, what you can do to ensure that you are trading successfully. Most mistakes that people make consist of not remembering the reality that the Forex market involves real cash.

This is extremely important and can quickly have your situation turning ugly really fast. If you slip and forget about the fact that you are dealing with real cash it will take no time at all before you are suddenly broke, and wondering where exactly things went wrong.

A much better option is to take the time to really review your choices. By doing this, not only can you ensure that you are well on your way towards success, but you can also ensure that you are working to slowly increase your options over time.

Many people rush into the Forex market and quickly discover that things are not turning out quite right. In order to really ensure that you make the right decisions it is important to realize just how disastrous things can really turn in the market.

Most consumers have no clue how the different currency rates can really impact aspects. It is very important to know and understand this. For example, if everyone who holds currency in the United States dollar started trying to dump their currency at the same time; this would force the value of the dollar into all-time lows.

However, at the same time, if everyone is trying to purchase the exact same type of currency this would again lead to people suddenly finding the value changing significantly. The biggest difference in this situation though would be the currency would go up significantly in value.

Taking the time to really understand how these things can impact is critical. Far too many people do not devote the time necessary to understanding these issues and quite quickly, they discover themselves in a situation that is not good for them. Taking the time to ensure you properly understand the Forex market before you ever start investing will help you to avoid dangerous situations that can really hurt your finances, or the finances of the world.

## In Conclusion

Forex trading can be fun as well as tremendously profitable, but in all honesty, it is always more fun when it is profitable.

In the examples you were shown you can see first-hand that trading Forex does not have to be complicated. Yes, it takes work and dedication, but all things which have huge potential rewards require work and dedication.

The rules, tips, and techniques laid out in this book are designed to lay the groundwork for you to trade successfully. Some of these are hard and fast rules that you definitely must not ignore.

Many of the hard and fast Forex trading rules have to do with discipline and risk control. Without these you simply cannot be successful. Even if you are exceptionally well capitalized you can easily make your account disappear without risk control.

If you do remain disciplined, properly capitalized, and risk aware, Forex trading offers you the opportunity of a lifetime. The leverage available in Forex combined with proper money management can grow a small trading account to levels of equity that you never thought were possible.

To Your Trading Success

**Market Research**

http://www.forextrading.com/

http://www.fxcm.com/

http://en.wikipedia.org/wiki/Foreign_exchange_market

http://www.forexfloor.com/

http://www.buzzle.com/articles/automated-forex-trading-system-does-it-work.html